The

Year

of the

Poet

July 2014

The Poetry Posse

inner child press, ltd.

The Poetry Posse

Jamie Bond

Gail Weston Shazor

Albert 'Infinite' Carrasco

Siddartha Beth Pierce

Janet P. Caldwell

June 'Bugg' Barefield

Debbie M. Allen

Tony Henninger

Joe DaVerbal Minddancer

Robert Gibbons

Neetu Wali

Shareef Abdur – Rasheed

Kimberly Burnham

William S. Peters, Sr.

General Information

The Year of the Poet
July Edition

The Poetry Posse

1st Edition : 2014

Publisher Information
1st Edition : Inner Child Press :
intouch@innerchildpress.com
www.innerchildpress.com

ISBN-13 : 978-0692248485 (Inner Child Press, Ltd.)
ISBN-10 : 069224848X

$ 12.99

Dedication

This Book is dedicated to

Poetry

&

the Spirit

of our Everlasting Muse.

Poets . . .
sowing seeds in the
Conscious Garden of Life,
that those who have yet to come
may enjoy the Flowers.

F oreword

Friends, Family and Readers

Here we are. We have just crossed over the Hump as The Poetry Posse. In month 7 our theme is Summer Fun, Joy and all those "Feel Good" things. I wish to thank each of the Poets for their contribution of verse and perspective. I think you will enjoy this one as you embrace the words of each soul and consider how does this apply or not to your own personal journey.

As we share our thoughts, there is a vicarious nature which we can embrace and thus broaden our own perspectives, dreams and visions as the possibilities manifest into being. Bottom line . . . enjoy your summer and the brightness that has been waiting for you to arrive.

Be sure to check out our internationally acclaimed Feature Poets to include Christena A. V. Williams from Jamaica, Dr. John R. Strum (Bob) from Australia and Kolade Olanrewaju Freedom from Nigeria . . . they each have a unique and prolific voice. . . . enjoy

Bless Up

Bill

SUMMER

Saunter at a snail's pace and still accomplish tasks

the Tired Caregiver

Preface

The year of the poet is a collectable collaboration of distinguished artists personally selected to write and publish every month affection ally donned as the poetry posse.

We are honored to have such an elite spectrum of "Pen Mates" along with spotlights of monthly features that you may not have otherwise been introduced to.

The books are all free downloads at inner child press for only 5 dollars for the physical copy. We have made these books affordable to the public, struggling artists, friends, fans and family.

We are proud to present this for your reading pleasure.

Enjoy,

Jamie Bond

Thank God for Poetry
otherwise
we would have a problem !

~ wsp

Table of Contents

Dedication   v

Foreword   vii

Preface   ix

The Poetry Posse

Jamie Bond   1

Gail Weston Shazor   9

Albert 'Infinite' Carrasco   21

Siddartha Beth Pierce   29

Janet P. Caldwell   37

June 'Bugg' Barefield   45

Debbie M. Allen   53

Tony Henninger   61

Joe DaVerbal Minddancer   69

Robert Gibbons   77

Neetu Wali   87

Shareef Abdur – Rasheed   95

Kimberly Burnham   103

William S. Peters, Sr.   111

Table of Contents . . . *continued*

July Features   119

Christena A. V. Williams   121

Dr. John R. Strum (Bob)   131

Kolade Olanrewaju Freedom   141

Other Anthological Works   151

Tee Shirts & Hats   175

Poets, Writers . . . know that we are the enchanting magicians that nourishes the seeds of dreams and thoughts . . . it is our words that entice the hearts and minds of others to believe there is something grand about the possibilities that life has to offer and our words tease it forth into action . . . for you are the Poet, the Writer to whom the Gift of Words has been entrusted . . .

~ wsp

poetry is . . .

The
Year
of the
Poet

July 2014

The Poetry Posse

inner child press, ltd.

Poetry succeeds where instruction fails.

~ wsp

Jamie Bond

Jamie Bond

Jamie Bond aka UnMuted Ink is an authoress, radio show hostess, poetess and spoken word maven.

She is; as she says "google-able" if you type in itsbondjamiebond or unmuted ink; you'll find her on various social networks. Born and raised in Brick City aka Newark, NJ. Jamie Bond has been recognized publicly by her peers in various genres for her poetic influences. Her Poetic resume is extensive and her spoken word performances go far beyond 1,000 stage appearances globally. Best known for her networking and marketing skills; her future goals are to become more grounded as a liaison for a variety of fundraisers, activism, volunteering as an advocate as she uses her pen and voice to empower and raise the consciousness of those around her.

Her Motto

Help me to help you to help us… BUT if helping you hurts me, then I can't help you!

http://www.facebook.com/IBJB.BrickCity

SUMMER

S-sweet
U-unforgettable
M-memories
M-manufacture
E-endless
R-reasons

I remember
summer fun and good times, house parties, fireworks,
lemonade. sweet tea, block parties and cook outs,
friends, laughs, games, bubble baths,
playing in the park, fireflies, climbing fences,
cartwheels, jumping rope, basketball, safe playgrounds,
dodge ball, hopscotch, football, riding my bike,
sunrises and sunsets, pen pals and music
pool halls and arcades
coming in when the street lights turned on,
swimming, camp, girl scouts,
skateboards, roller skating rinks,
packed car to drive ins, the beach,
eating easy meals as a family
hotdogs, hamburgers, mac nd cheese were my favorites
summer scent of fresh linen on a clothesline,
Saturday morning cartoons, one tv in the living room,
visiting my grandma, crafts, poetry, traveling, reading
siblings, cousins, family and friends,
I remember summer love and loving summer
Never wanting it to end.....

Saunter at a snail's pace and still accomplish tasks

The squirrels were playing today
Right before my eyes
Last night I could've sworn
That I saw a few fireflies
I was waiting patiently for a change
And I actually heard a breeze
As I looked up into the sky
I acknowledged the green tree leaves

The air smells so good today
A combination of sweet good things
Today is an awakening for me
For I can even hear my own heart beat

Lawn mowers, birds singing,
Even a plane overhead not far
Things that have been here all along
And I'm hearing them from inside the car

What kind of mood am I in today?
That my body allowed me to relax like this
Surely I've heard all of these things before
But today I'm more appreciative of it

Let me walk slowly and still get things done
That's all I ever asked of my higher self these days

The exhausted caregiver

From here to there I'm not sure I care
My job could send me anywhere
Don't they screen these nuts I get stuck with?
What's wrong with them?
I don't know about this

One wishes they were dead and so do I
The other counts the days they don't die
One of them even got upset
Because I put the wash on permanent press
Tried to argue that it's not a dryer
Now I wonder why I bother

Sometimes I walk in
And they're too uptight from last night
Complaining about their families
As if I could ever make it alright
I have compassion for each one
Don't get me wrong
But I'm only there for a few hours
I haven't been there all along

I'm starting to feel tired
Before I start my day
And actually I'd stay home
If I didn't need the pay
Nurse; can help can you help me?
Can you do me a favor dear?
Everyone could use my services
But what would they do if I weren't there

I'm flattered that they need me so much
As if I'm the salt of the earth
But my path to life
Has been mapped out for me
Since way before my birth

Jamie Bond

Gail

Weston

Shazor

This is a creative promise ~ my pen will speak to and for the world. Enamored with letters and respectful of their power, I have been writing for most of my life. A mother, daughter, sister and grandmother I give what I have been given, greatfilledly.

Author of . . .

"An Overstanding of an Imperfect Love"

available at Inner Child Press.

www.facebook.com/gailwestonshazor

www.innerchildpress.com/gail-weston-shazor

navypoet1@gmail.com

Flavorful Days

Summer tastes like the ocean
Salty and wet on the tongue
Breezy and easy on the eyes
Warm
The wind lifts my skirts tails
To see if I indeed
Have the bee's knees
Hidden beneath
And what is found is as sweet as honey

Summer tastes like mangoes
Growing wild on the streets
The uncultured goodness
Is never polite or kind
In its beckoning forth of your hand
Untamed, it too belongs to no one
Free
Bountifully sweet
My kisses are ripe

Summer tastes like coconuts
Round and firm and high
Upon trees
With draping and showy leaves
Covering the full milkiness
That one might dare
To risk life and limb
Just to obtain a taste
The flesh is sweet

Summer tastes like ice cream
Melting down my chin
And I can't lick it fast enough
To keep it off my fingers
Sweet and sticky
Laughing at the mess we have made
I place your fingers in my mouth
Only to find that you now
Flavor my tongue

Summer tastes like heat
A warmth of heart and hand
The look in your eyes
When you come through the screen
Hot
And I have been waiting clothed
In a summer dress
Fan blowing in the window
On a summer's eve

No Socks

I

Sit here

With my feet

In the warm sand

Join me in this place

And let's talk about life

Maybe ours together

Definitely the time apart

See, we don't need socks in this season

Summer is the time to create our years

Latitude 18

And the sun is hot in this latitude
In this latitude of summer
I find some shade
Under the Noni tree
Its medicinal leaves
Healing the welts
Of one too long in the darkness

The babies play at the edge of the water
At the edge of the water
Just this side of safeness
In and out they run
They laugh as if the very music
Is being snatched out the air
And bounced off the cliffs

My eyelids grow heavy with the watching
Heavy with the watching of play
Cymbals tingle and lull
Deeper into the sand
Until I am wrapped in the sound
Of comfortable snoozing
Here on this beach

Hurricane Season

The new storms have been named
And I find it amazing still
It is always in the feminine
That we anticipate disaster
And it may be true that women
Underscore the pain
Rended upon other women
And a breaking heart breaks a heart
Storms come unexpectedly
Even if you clothe yourself in love
Lightening slashes and thunder roils
And I smell the dampness
Lingering under green leaves
It is in this minute, in these wee hours
That I cling onto the only words I can hear
"I love you"
And they vanish in the storm
Tomorrow vanishes in the storm
I wait for God to calm this storm
That threatens to rend me in pieces
To dry the tears that melts the light
And clouds into the grey
Instead he calms me
My doubts, my fears
Holds me close in His peace
While the storm rages
And how could I have understood
That I could not have wished
This love into the eye of a hurricane
For she could not have destroyed
What belongs to Him

In the sand, there is black rain
In the sand I am black rain
In the sand I am silent
And sometimes I find it hard to breathe
I can't swallow
These storms have no name
This summer I don't fear the rain
I am not scared of the feminine
The breaking apart creates new spaces
Places for me to grow
Places for you to know
And even in storms God is close
And even in the rain God is near
My love is steady
For it wasn't the storm that was my enemy
Being alone in my storm was
The wind has ceased it's howling
And soon you will hear me
For he named me and
He controls the she
That we have given voice to
And I wait quietly and without fear because
All storms must answer to Him
And He provides the blessing in each one

Sundressed

In yellows and pinks
Eye lets my eye roam
Through the dark timbers of
Cottoned mahogany trees
And it's hard to keep pace
With their constant movements
Even through half closed lids
My fingers enjoy the blaze of color
Against a midday sun
The branches reach down
To hold tomorrow
As it giggles and races away
It is always by the water
That they in man groves gather
Tasting supple, limber and smooth
Here I await them always
Colorful and patterned Afrika
And there is nothing
That can hide their beauty
I love them more than breathing
So patiently I await
The small ministrations of life
The crowned legacy of hues
That is now sundress season

Hydration

Water hydrants shoot skyward
And we run headfirst into the spray
Screaming and shouting
So the neighbors can hear
None of us own bathing suits
So we pull the legs of our shorts
As high as we can
For this brief cleansing

Young mothers carry babies into
Our own city Jordan
And it is not for the babies
But for themselves
So that they can remember the feel
Of before responsibility
Far too young for such a burden
And yet here they are
On the same street they grew up on
Breasts barely full
Waiting on angel to touch them
Seal their lips with salvation

Nothing this good ever lasts
And we can hear the sirens of
The water and power trucks coming
So we all dance harder
And twirl faster
So not one inch of us is dry
Mothers begin to come out
To gather their own
Back onto hard, dry, hot stoops
Carrying whatever raggedy toweling
They can muster up on such short notice

It's Saturday
And the fire hydrant has been breached
So now we must return to walk ups
And hope the fan is on in the windows
One by one we are cleaned
Greased and in pajamas
We are sat between knees with
Combs and hair grease
Tomorrow we will hear about
Crossing the river
But today we already been in Jordan.

Albert

Infinite

Carrasco

Albert Carrasco writes hieroglyphics encrypted in poetic form. His linguistics are not the norm. When it comes to wisdom, sleet ,rain snow and hail its a lyrical storm. He's pure like Fiji, he got the power to hear the dead with no auji. For living a life so tabu, He learnt a die-a-lect , his mouth moves... But at times it's the voice of the crossovers coming through. When he's on stage he has a body temp of 98 degrees... When He recites you feel this chilling breeze, hair stands on skin when he's in the avatar state of his kin. He's non traditional, an unorthodox outspoken urban individual that lived through the subliminal, now he's back to give guidance to his people.

Infinite the poet 2014

Infinite poetry @lulu.com
Alcarrasco2 on YouTube
Infinite the poet on reverbnation

The Poems this month are from my Book
Infinite Poetry
available at
http://www.lulu.com/us/en/shop/al-infinite-carrasco/infinite-poetry/paperback/product-21040240.html

Rooftops

I used to go to the tallest building in the projects as a kid to stare at the passing planes, Then close my eyes and pretend I was in first class , clapping my hand like the rich do on television, as to let the stewardess know with out words to refill my wine glass, instead of me standing on melted tar, I imagined myself rich flying to a destination, smoking a cigar, maybe to the Caribbean or maybe bogota, or start talking funny like ohh lala wee, that's me talking French walking around Paris, with a rich man poodle with name brand sunglasses, Louie v with gucci sandals, able to buy what I want where I want with no hassles, I pictured myself the owner of a house so big it looked like a castle, gave me such a thrill, sometimes I forgot I was on the roof of the " boot" a nycha building in castle hill, my friends used to make believe they were soldiers and pretended to shoot the plane down, not me, I wondered from where this plane came, was it coming was it going?, did it come from somewhere sunny? or was it snowy? Does anyone on that plane know me? Na I wouldn't be that lucky, around me your lucky just to have a b I k e, The closes thing for me flying on a plane, was to fly my k i t e, I used to stand on the roof for hours, stood out later than the birds and squirrels , I used to run home so I didn't break curfew and get in trouble, if I did it was worth it, because without leaving the Bronx I traveled the world on a rooftop, as a poor little kid.

My joy is giving

I love you all,
I wish I can be everywhere at once
So I can enjoy y'all,
I wish I can take pieces of my heart and spread it out,
Give my family a piece,
Give my friends a piece
Give my fans a piece
Ill make sure I leave a piece to the lost ones in the streets,
They need to be loved by somebody,
I'm not gonna push em to the side like society did me.
I want to lift heads when they're down,
I want to tell a single parent that they'll be alright although
the mother/ father never comes around.
I want to tell the hurting, that I feel their pain,
I want the ones that feel ugly to fell beautiful,
And I'm not talking about appearance.
I want to give the poor wealth,
The sick health.
If i could...The dead breath.
I just want to give and do,
To you all... Infinite loves you.

Every day it's hot

You hear the sound of four wheelers and dirt bikes
On local roads unpaved

You can hit the beaches in isla verde
Con mi gientes
And ride the waves

At nite you see the punto ochos
And the corollas carrying on
Listening to reggae tong
Looking tight

Hollering at the freaky tonas
Although I prefer
Mark anthonys otra nota

I can nude bathe in the back of my house
In a hammock
Or lay on a sabanna on the floor

Gaze up at the steamy skies
Or stare at the trees
Watching mangos fall

Wake up in the mornings
To the beat of plena
Or the smell of cinnamon
Being stored in avena

The dialect I hardly hear in new York
Is the basic language you hear
When my people's talk
And that's Spanish

Carne guisado or arroz con pollo
A famous tradition
When a Spanish woman is in the kitchen
And what's on the table
Before we say grace

I'm taking a trip to the mother land
I miss my people and my culture
I'm going back to my place

Puerto Rico, my home.

Siddartha

Beth

Pierce

Siddartha Beth Pierce is a Mother, Poet, Artist and African and Contemporary Art Historian. Her art, poetry and teaching were featured on PBS in April 2001 while she was the Artist-in-Residence and Associate Professor at Virginia State University in Petersburg, Virginia. She received her BA in Studio Art from George Mason University in Fairfax, Virginia and her M.A.E. from Virginia Commonwealth University in Richmond, Virginia. She continued into PhD. Studies in African and Contemporary Art studies at Virginia Commonwealth University where she is now All but Dissertation. Her works of poetry and art have been featured in numerous newspaper articles, journals, magazines and chapbooks.

http://www.innerchildpress.com/siddartha-beth-pierce.php

http://www.youtube.com/watch?v=OQ87NrLt_to

http://www.writerscafe.org/Siddartha

Mother Earth

Summer's warmth seeps into my soul
The sun's rays, dressed in gold
As shadows dance among the leaves
A cloak of heat enraptures me,
So Divine
That you may find
Within the day's of summer's strength
As mighty as any beast
That travels along the trails
About this old farm house
Bears, birds, badgers, fox alike
Alight in day and night
Within the dressing of the hot months
That have come
To please us with the light of Father Sun
Then cool us in the midnight air
La Lune on high, a lonely pair
Of celestial beings delighting all
Us creatures, here below
On Mother Earth in blue-green glow.

Outside My Open Window

The pages flutter by
As words escape my eyes
I am taken to dream
A beautiful scene
Where upon my lips
I feel a delightful kiss
Yet alone, in this bed, I rest.

Who has haunted me this eve
Blessed me with sweet love
Only an Angel from above
Could have passed this feeling to me
Or twas it only a dream.

A lover of old perhaps
Has come back to me again
To cleanse me of impurity
Place a smile upon my skin
With the sweet grasping that I feel
Towards him.

I wonder what I might have been
To have ever felt such longing
For a true love, in reality,
But twas only a dream
Or was it a haunting
Subliminally met between two worlds
Apart, yet, united as One
Beneath the moon's glow
Outside my open window.

The Deweeding

A whisper
A dandelion seed
Glides gently
Upon the breeze.

Wafting
Waiting
For someone
To snag it-
Wish upon
And set it free-
With the gentle
Blow of
Their sweet breath.

Scented
Desperately-
The stench of tobacco
And the fear of the
Gasping
Lion's head-
Left behind
Once it was tugged

Roughly from its
Grassy mane.

A day's work unfurled
And
Glid
Upon
Until tomorrow.
When again the
Sun arises
And the dirty toil
Begins once more.

.

Janet

Perkins

Caldwell

Janet wrote her first poems and short stories in an old diary where she noted her daily thoughts. She wrote whether suffering, joyful or hoping for peace in the world. She started this process at the tender age of Eight. This was long before journaling was in vogue.

Along with her thoughts, poetry and stories, she drew what she refers to as Hippie flowers. Janet still to this day embraces the Sixties and Seventies flower power symbol, of peace and love, which are a very important part of her consciousness.

Janet wrote her first book, in those unassuming diaries, never to be seen by the light of day due to an unfortunate house fire. This did not deter her drive. She then opted for a new batch of composition journals and filled everyone. In the early nineteen-eighties, Janet held a byline in a small newspaper in Denton, Texas while working full time, being a Mother and attending Night School.

Since the early days Janet has been published in newspapers, magazines and books globally. She also has enjoyed being the feature on numerous occasions, both in Magazines, Radio and on a plethora of Sites. She has gone on to publish three books. *5 degrees to separation* 2003, *Passages* 2012 and her latest book *Dancing Toward the Light . . . the journey continues* 2013. All of her Books are available through Inner Child Press along with Fine Book Stores Globally. Janet P. Caldwell is also the Chief Operating Officer of Inner Child ltd.

http://www.janetcaldwell.com/

http://www.innerchildpress.com/janet-p-caldwell.php

https://www.facebook.com/JanetPCaldwell

Our Street

Remembering back . . .
to those sweet summers
as a child. Most of our
parents were at work
to put bread on the table
and my, my, my
how we ran free and wild.

Every summer, *someone* always
busted the fire hydrants
which gave us a temporary reprieve
from the summer's scorching heat.

At the middle of our street
the pavement was low
causing a swirling
pushing, rushing, swooshing
and heavenly pool
of gushing H2O.

And no one, I mean
not a soul, ever told.
Though we knew
who had done the deed.
He was our hero
and in our memories
this *boy* remains so.

Kids ran hard from every domicile
just to twirl, giggle and dance in the spray.
Letting the water douse our faces.
We stripped our clothes until all that was left
were under – weared bodies
as the sweat and grime left us
never leaving *those* parental traces.

Heck, some got knocked down
from the water's force.
We didn't care though
as the water *tended*
to more than scraped knees
it washed us *clean*.
Anything . . .
anything to *beat* the *heat*
on our tree lined street.

All Will be Known

Happiness has represented a lot of things for me.
People, places and a cure for a much loved one
that seemed out of reach and now enjoyed.

Riding the bus on the East Coast, finally
catching a train and one day ended up
with the man that loves me *true*
for three weeks in Puerto Rico.
I shall never remain the same.

Happiness is a walk on the beach
hand in hand . . . talking
and *really looking* at people
at times, staring at the sun;
and finally a crescent moon winked
with the sand between our toes.

A picnic shared on a coffee table
with prayers offered to something
bigger than ourselves.
We should not consume this food
but we giggled and did it our way
just for today, just for this day
after all we never remained the same.

It is also those glorious *summer storms*
as the thunder and lightening excite, to let us know.
"I am here today and will blow away tomorrow
to the world at last . . . as the *Gods*
exhibit a colorful rainbow shown to every nation."
Something I have always loved and wanted.

Love and peace among the peoples
nothing or no – one hidden
all will be known.

Joy Comes in all Colors

My lover

my children

my grandchildren

and friends

bring joy untold.

Just ask me

and I'll tell you.

Joy comes in all colors.

I ought to know.

June
'Bugg'
Barefield

June 'Bugg' Barefield

June Barefield ~ Poet-Activist-Teacher-Author

Born and raised in the Midwest, currently residing in East St Louis, IL. June's interests include long walks, sunrises, cheesecake, and words. He considers the NRA, and it's supporters 2B a 21st century Nazi-ism! The author of two collections of poetry which include B4 the Dawn, and The Journeyman

I B. Self educated, and proud to be humbled. An avid reader, and teacher, counselor in his community at what we as a society have termed "at risk children". June refers to them as Gang members, and dope dealers. A brilliant speaker, and motivator; fluent in at least three religions! June's favorite quote: "FUCK THE SYSTEM!"

for booking call : 720 404 8563

http://authorsdb.com/authors-directory/2292-june-barefield

you can get more of June here . . .

https://www.facebook.com/JuneBugg900

https://www.facebook.com/june.barefield.7

http://www.innerchildpress.com/june-barefield.php

the BADDLANDS

I stand
I see it
In awe of it
this..,
This nameless place
salted with iron rich cinders
I close my eyes
I imagine
this place
casted long ago
by some ancient river
worn away b y forces from under
Torn then ripped
by wind and water
And to that long passed
a twisted trunk of Juniper
still Stands

The Baddlands they call you
for want
for not

The Baddlands
the land that time forgot
I can see patterns
like fingerprints
bleached, cracked, and scorched
The desert soil
in net like patterns
dizzying, yet flattering
brilliant and blue is the sky
magnificent red crimson
sands of earth

The Baddlands
R U cursed?
nursed briefly by a spatter of raindrops
creating a ditch
so suddenly a small stream appears
it seems in seconds
to disappear
NOW SILENCE
miles upon miles
filled to the brim
this silence
Can you hear it?
There it is again
crashing in upon you
The silence
the prairie dog
and oriole
the rattlesnake
and rabbit bush
They hear it
in silence
Raggedy and rugged
worn down by wind
then rain
and time
Oh how timeless you seem
with respect
in awe
My souls screams!
IN SILENCE 4
the baddlands...

The 1st Gift

Fragrance them say
the first gift
Ancient & mysterious
myth them say
Miraculous
With God Supreme moving moons
& planets
Stars & earth
Commanding craters
Rolling over humongous boulders
Laying paradise out in layers
this fragrance
Rising from the waters
From this great abyss, her island tropics came to exist
This fragrance lifts as clouds drift above
a purple mist, married to a sweet heavenly kiss on volcanic
heights
slowly they shift from lip to neck
sipping waterfalls
As lightning strikes, and thunder rolls, and twists
the Fragrance them say...
The First Gift.

STILLNESS

Just B4 the Dawn it's calm
At dusk it's just as wonderful
But by this time folk to worked up 2 notice the beautiful
LOTUS plant
Can't grow if U don't know
this truth...
What U call GOD is all about you
He - She is you
But U partnered up with the world
Privy to all the motion that death, and destruction's
unfurled...
Take 0NE step to the rear
Can U hear
that SILENCE?
Place this silence inside of U
It will follow you
THIS silence...
In spIrit & in tRuth....

Debbie
M.
Allen

Debbie M. Allen is a Pennsylvania native that has remained true to her passion for the love of poetry. She has always had a passion for poetry. In 2010 she took that passion and made it her cause, always maintaining the truth of her experiences and the beliefs she holds dear.

Debbie is the Author of "A Poet Never Dies," her first book of poetry which was published in 2012. Since then she has published her second book of poems, "The Spiral of a Pisces: In Manic Flow," which encompasses her ever spiraling transition of expression. She can be found participating in various avenues of spoken word and poetry under the pseudonym D. Flo'essence including The Truth Commission Movement, Penology Ink Productions, Jersey Radical Productions and What's The News.

The Secret to Peace

I have found peace…
Overflowing…
Flooding solitude with open arms
An embrace into loving light
Tightly wounding me
In the press of inner might…
Abounding in joyous sounds
That has finally led me home…
After wondering if this dome
I created to shelter sanity
Would actually crack me as I roamed
Alone in circles…
But I quickly learned if circles can devote so much time to
360 degrees of hopeless grind…
I can convert its center to anchor me,
Tranquility in knowing…
Calm never ceases in the mind,
Although it sometimes settles like a mime…
Mimicking life's movements
Like prime directives to fake out emotions…
Pitch joy into oceans leaving us pirating
For ages…just for grins and giggles
To pass the hard times away…

But I have found the secret to peace's stay…

Smile as broad as muscles will allow
Before the ache sets in…and if it does
Count that ache as a win
Lingering so you won't forget what gladness feels like…

Laugh as much as vocals can expel
To hinder any dwelling sadness
Trying to steal way with bliss

Kiss worries goodbye every night
Deeply…
So if you shall meet them again it will know that love was
Beautiful to even the roughest of times

I found peace…
An easy mind…
An easy mind…
An easy…mind…

Happiness Finds Me

There are those moments I peep through
Inner madness
And the sunshine grabs this wandering soul of mines…
Takes me in the rays
In beam…in bright displays
Of lingering memories…
Those days when there was nothing but happiness that
found me…
Warm in waves of smiles
It's been awhile but I remember…

There are those moments I see through rainy skies
Beyond tear filled eyes
And water is the healer to bruised hearts
Rinsing me in streams
In dreams…that anything
Can survive what storms may bring in its aftermath
A casting out of lonesome life
Just to dance with raindrops
That never stops for awkward beats…
I remember the deep heat of sun showers…

There are those moments that joy screams through
The chill of snow…
Beautiful flakes that shake me free
From sad times…binding thoughts with the wings of
Snow angels…rearranging the angles of friendship
Just me, the cold and
Yet it's magical to hold onto…

There are those moments happiness finds me…
Especially when I'm not looking…

F. U. N.

Freely…
Throw inhibitions into the tornado
So you know there will be no way for it to
Track you down…
Can't go walking around
Worrying about what your face looks like
On the roller coaster of life…
"Silliness is the best freedom of expression"
Yes…I just made that lesson up
And yup…I'm smiling to myself right now…

Understand…
There are no rules to engage
Any circumstance…
For instance…formal dances that turn into
Nonsense prances along the dance floor
Just because you decided two left feet
Was more enticing to the funny bone instead of a left and a
right
Or staying up all night
Over glasses of wine that over time
Gets you mumbling about all the dumb things you did
As a child…
Shit was wild back then…

Never…
Allow the mind to trick you into believing that growing up
Means that fun ceases
Causing the stumble into preaches…
"That's not for adults"
Give in already…
There's a time for being steady
And ohh so many hours to just act out!
Who cares what people think…
I know and am very educated in the art of
Not giving two fucks during the brink of
Chaotic, fantastically busting madness…

Ok, is this good advice?
The hell if I know…
I'm just enjoying the spilling of non-consequential words…
Unless of course I decide to put it to action…
Speaking of this…
I just remembered I'm about to miss
My sky dive into a tryst
With self-gratification and pure silliness…
Hope you enjoy your fun…I will!

Tony Henninger

Tony has been writing for about 20 years. He has published one book titled " A Journey of Love." He has also contributed to several Anthologies. His book is available at Innnerchild Press and Amazon.com.

You can find him at Facebook.com/Tony Henninger

Linkdin.com/Tony Henninger or

tonyhenninger@yahoo.com

Song Of The Ocean

On a warm summer day,
I found a secluded spot,
while walking on the beach.
A quiet place, in the shade,
between some moss-covered rocks
where the sounds of everyday life could not reach.
I began listening, intently, to
the song of the ocean.
Closing my eyes, I felt,
my heart being filled with many emotions.
A song of contentment,
of serenity,
calm and yet, strong.

My heart fluttered as the music
entered my soul and I began to hum.
Swaying to the sound I, slowly,
opened my eyes to see
the myriad colors of the sun's rays
glistening on the water
as the waves kissed the shore.
The joy of the ocean's song
filled with so much life.
My heart bursting with delight
at seeing such a magnificent sight.

How blessed I am to be alive,
How blessed I am to hear,
the song of the ocean
urging me to come near,
to come back home.

Beyond Limitations

My heart is pounding wildly
as I run along the beach
of the Sea of Serenity.
Trying to escape the
outstretched hands of loss,
of regret, of conformity.
Saying to myself,
"There is more beyond what my eyes see."

I stop and turn and face them
as the moist sand between my toes
gives me the strength to stand.
And the waves coming ashore
offer me more,
saying to me,
"Come with us!"
"There is more beyond the sea!"

Looking inside myself,
I see, my soul radiating.
Blinding me like the light
of the mid-summer sun.
Its warmth sending out love,
penetrating everyone.
Saying to me,
"There is more beyond the light!"

So, I dive in with a grin,
accepting the invitation,
coming to the realization,
saying to myself,
"There is more beyond my limitations!"

A Song Of Joy And Happiness

A song of Joy and Happiness
is all I want to sing.
To release the words from my soul,
a change to the world to bring.

A song of Love and Hope,
of Freedom from despair.
A Blessing just to be alive
with so much Love to share.

A song so Beautiful and Divine
to make us all aware.
To open our eyes and not be blind.
For each other to respect and care.

A song of Compassion and Unity
to bring us together as One.
To make this world the paradise
wished for by everyone.

A song of Joy and Happiness
is what I want everyone to sing.
Release the words from your lips.
A change to the world can begin.

"SING WITH ME…."

Dance

As I whirl and dance

in my Beloved's romance

everything falls away.

Come dance with me

on the floor of the skies.

Let the universe see

the love in your eyes.

Dance in the rain,

wash away the pain

and clear your soul

that you might realize

the fire of the sun

burning in everyone.

Tony Henninger

Joe
Da Verbal
MindDancer

Joseph L Paire' aka Joe DaVerbal Minddancer . . .
is a quiet man, born in a time where civil liberties
were a walk on thin ice. He's been a victim of his
own shyness often sidelined in his own quest for
love. He became the observer, charting life's path.
Taking note of the why, people do what they do.
His writings oft times strike a cord with the
dormant strings of the reader. His pen the rosined
bow drawn across the mind. He comes full-frontal
or in the subtlest way, always expressing in a way
that stimulate the senses.

https://www.facebook.com/joe.minddancer

The Beach

Waves crashed along the sandy shore
Footprints erased and were no more
Broken shells fish scales a tattered sail
Remnants of a boat that didn't fair too well
Pylons cast shadows neath the boardwalk
The setting Sun reaches out before dark

Where's my blanket and my drink?
Where's the drudgery and city stink?
Lost in this rising tide; I think
As my beautiful shoreline begins to shrink
Sea birds call out in the order of a choir
Flickering flames and embers from a fire

The sights the sounds;
The smell of an oceanic breeze
A taste of salt in the air I breathe
Such things as these remind me of summer
Reminds me of the snow I was buried under
Now it's just bare feet in the sand.
Trying to even out this farmers tan

Oh ocean blue, oh starry night
Give me your peace.
Grant me the solitude of your calm
And with the wave of your palm
I'll sleep with the comfort of your beach.

Cooking Cards And Cussing

The yard was abuzz with shrill screams
Little ones laughing and playing
It seems as though the day would never end for them.
For us it was necessary to have a moment.
A gathering if you will of friends and family
 Dad was going to breakout his new grill!

His silly Hawaiian shirt, socks on with sandals
It was a time to relax and enjoy.
Charcoal smoke, cigarettes and weed
The teens stepped back into the trees
Trying to lose that scent in the breeze
A call to spades, the elders yelled, bid whist
It was on, as the table was set.
Three brand new packs of bicycle decks.

Coolers filled with beer, little hugs and water
Dad rocked that grill, fall of the bone ribs
Just like they ought'a, citronella candles flickered.
The music played loud, old school and new school
The kids danced for the crowd.
Old Butch shouted out; that ain't dancing
What are y'all doing? He grabbed Miss Sally
They started grooving, hand dancing to the beat
 They were light on their feet,
Old Butch could barely breathe
Sally damn near lost her weave.
We were rolling with laughter
down on our knees.

A crowd formed around the table
The game had got intense,
The women paired up, oh the suspense!
A little fussing a lot of cussing
A lot of trusting their partner, the game went on
They played a little harder. They took it serious
Playing fast and furious,
We were curious of how it would end.
They broke out in laughter
They ran a Boston on them.
NEXT; was the cry, a new team set down.
These Sisters wasn't about to give up that crown.

There were conversations everywhere
A few snuck moments of passion.
It was an impromptu outing,
These things kept the family lasting.
These times were a highlight
Dotted out throughout the summer
Never ruined by the sound of thunder
An occasional fight usually over nothing
The laughter never stopped,
not even the next day.
Phone calls abound giving out the play by play.

Plans were in the making for another soiree'
The fun of summer we wanted to have every day.

The Second Half

The ball drops for the NEW YEAR
I drop just in time for the second tier.
July marks the month of my birth
To be precise it's on the first.
It's the beginning of my summer
It's my relief from slumber, my water slide.
Pride takes the form of a smile.
While the days light, lasts until ten.
While the days heat is still lingering
We played softball, and ran.
Laid blankets out in the park
Drank of wine and inhaled the fine hemp.
During the month of July, there is no dark.

Mornings filled with the sound of birds
A brief moment of cool air as dawn opens up.
The fun is in the suns rise, the fun is in the knowing.
The fun is showing a child a good time
Ice cream cones and shaved ice flavored lime
Sparklers and firecrackers,
Fishing poles and night crawlers
We get it in we bout it bout it
Everyday is a celebration, every week a vacation
Maybe once during a storm we chill;
It's still relaxation, tire swings and rollercoaster's
Cabins by the lake, all these joyous things
Is what my summer makes.

Robert
Gibbons

Robert Gibbons moved to New York City in the summer of 2007 in search of his muse-Langston Hughes. Robert has performed all over New York City.

His first collection of Poetry, Close to the Tree was published by Threes Rooms Press and can be purchased at :

www.threeroomspress.com

You may contact Robert
via his FaceBook presences :

www.facebook.com/anthonyrobertgibbons

www.facebook.com/jamesmercerlangstonhughes

a garden

the rain falls

foreword

the world

a-crying garden

becoming

snow-in-summer

petals smothering

her ground swell

white frosting

only hear

the movement

the hanging baskets

taste- the- mint

the clove

only bee there

it seems as though

the garden

is phantasmagoric

painting Eden

an utopia

can not pansy

drawn in

by Edward Pothast's color

feel like

I make an impact

the impressionist sit

in silent cacophony

as audible enough

just fallible, too

the world is crying

as I read too much

look for the subtext

the nexus of my knees

as hard as the rock gardens

with the collection of snails

that brings me there.

clean up my act

the day will not be so de rigeur
there are two weeks of front lawns
have almost forgotten the smell
of fresh cut grass, the harassment of
weeds struggling to survive; this hedge
on this ledge of a mountain, but the
trees continue to whisper to Jesus
as fingers embark on a journey
the sun making skin bristle
rake and underbrush the plastic
bags.

and just because I am here
I taper like the red maple
next door, I wish I could
steal all of this, the flooring
of the walnut with its
collection of summer-house
green hulls and then crack
this open, miss the feeding
of sweat and the red- breasted
keeping watch over me
as this swatter of bugs
collecting bites gutting me
in this mackerel sky.

a summer ride somewhere near Boston

the turn off Bascom Road has the smell of dead
leaves and decomposing trees; it cold down here
on this summer road to Hades; instead of digging
up earthworms; we track the mirth; run into an army
of mosquitoes; a storm of palmetto bugs sabotaging
our arms; feel like razor wires, in this dark
canopy; just antiphony and skeletal remains;
marks the territory; the forest is invisible black
like a man pulling the plug in Brooklyn, but this
trail has never seen a sidewalk or traffic cop, only
lily pads with blossoms; even the air's been accosted
maybe a skunk; something rustling behind the bushes
but its obtuse; it protrudes behind this shack
even the grass is on a prowl with its
rusty scissor edges, but you better leave before dark
marshy water and liquid landscape swallow
both sides of the road; the mud quick sands;
the barren trees pitchfork out this dead see;
blue herons send chills; there are hidden trails
like dirty fingernails; scratch the surface.

a piece of Spring

" and now and then
    a fledgling cried,
    like destitute folk
    on the wayside." (after e.e. cummings)

the   dinner was late yesterday; after the visitation of a
friend; I think he really needed me to visit; home alone on
one of these holidays that tend to promote family, but I
would visit this person regardless if it is a holiday or not,
but I did, taking along with me a baguette, pate and some
expensive pickles; and we had a party for him; a few of us
sitting around reading e.e. cummings; and other poets we
admire, I bought a book of his poem off a bookstand for
one dollar; and it amazes me how a one dollar book can
contain so much power; like when cummings says," each
has his tastes but as for I;" "I like a certain party," and he is
correct; I do like a certain party; this person needed
company on a day like yesterday; a day when people are
parading back and forth with large packages of flowers and
fruit basket; so I deemed it necessary to bring the party to
him; to have an e.e. cummings party; I am so glad that
cummings uses the lower cases; I rather be more intimate
on day like yesterday; I was not quite sure how long I
would be there; but the time was well spent, but cummings
had more to say before I left; " it was the first ride and
believe I, we was happy," why not, we were happy, instead
he says we was, maybe because I and the we, maybe we
just happened to get together randomly and not sure how it
would end or even how it would start, but I, we did; I and
we, felt the same way, my family is far away from here;
and although I wanted to be with them I could not; I and
we was in the moment; I and we ate the baguette; and the
country pate; it was the I and we was; " acted right up to

the last minute;" cummings just read my mind; he really took over the party; in all his reserve; in all unscheduled agenda; I and we had a blast; I try to consider the life of the other; here is another visit I made with a friend to a convalescent home and this is what I saw; thanks to e.e. cummings in small letters; the small can be even more powerful:

~ * ~

when I walk into rehab
on the corner of Dean and Hoyt
the room opened its arms to me
as if Mary stands here;
the clerk becomes a deacon
ushering me upstairs
to the second floor
it becomes an upper room
I see old people
people that tell stories
with worry lines
and a hundred chances
to be disable
people who have seen
some of the great wars
the depression, the regret
of the generation;
people who are geriatric
unprotected; probably receiving
their social and their security
with a once a month check;
people with craters in their faces
once with the glory of the maker,
but the hater of a carpal,
a symptom, the criminality
of the elderly people;

who gives candy to their
grandchildren; may have been
members of a jury; people
once sugar daddies that lost
their cane and now the latter
rain is all that's left;

as I left the room
the weeping and the noisy;
the cold and the cozy,
wheelchairs around the
space; the place becomes
a purgatory of thought;
the graying moss of their
hair pull back behind scars;
as I lowered myself
to the street
there is no relief insight;
only the plight of living
hoping when the time
comes for me to enter
the upper room
someone like you
will be there

e.e. cummings, tells me, "a man who fallen among thieves
lay by the roadside on his back," so what should I do, but
give him some consolation; a man that is an elder; a man
with a cane; a man that would feed me from his table; I
could not be more thankful than this; be there for some one
in greater need than myself; it is not wealth; it is worthy; it
is reason cummings says, what's beyond logic happens
beneath will; nor can these moments be translated."

Neetu
Wali

Hi! I am Neetu. Who am I? This question is very difficult to answer.

Well! If you insist, let me reveal. I am a human and like every other human I eat, sleep, drink, dance, sing, laugh, smile, cry and so on. Hang on! There is a difference. Unlike most of the human beings, I breathe and when I breathe, I relax. When I am relaxed, I draw. I draw sketches of me in words.

I have been orbiting around sun for forty years now. I started this journey on the Valentine day of 1974. I have seen people craving for heaven and I was born in the only heaven on earth (Kashmir). My Grandfather was a spiritual personality and a renowned poet of his time. Though he left me around 35 years ago, I couldn't let him go. I carry him in my eyes and mind and will do that till the end of my life. I hate words, yet I am full of words. I know words cannot express, yet I express me through words, because they are the only medium I am familiar with. That is why I try to express me as much as possible with as minimum words as possible.

When I did Masters in business administration, I never knew, writing will be the only business in my life. More than hobby writing is a necessity for me, because it helps me get the load of thoughts off my head. I don't remember when it that I wrote my first poem was. But I surely know the time of my last poem. Surely, not before my last breath.

Summers Are Here

Summers are here
Frozen hearts of earth
Have begun to melt
The season is here
Season of warmth
Warmth of compassion
Darkness takes a break
Those sleeping awake
Summers are faith
Make mountains move
Oceans get rich
Days earn gold
Nights turn bold

Summers make you taste
The salt of your soul
Days gain weight
Nights lose height
Summers loosen nerves
Give strength to act
Summers mean light
Life becomes bright
Summers are hot!
Hot is cool
Hot is in

Summers are in
Everybody is hot

Sky is silent
earth is silent
Stars are silent
Planets are silent
oceans are silent
trees are silent
mountains are silent
woods are silent
winds are silent
silence is the nature of nature
When summers are here

Innocence

She was so simple
Yet her face had a glow
Her genuine and pure smile
That stuck to her lips every moment
And seemed dutiful to her
Made her more beautiful
Every guy looked at her
With eyes full of desire
Wanted to feel her skin
How many of them approached her
What they got in response
Was just a genuine smile
How could she explain
The reason of her glow
Ignorance can never
Understand innocence

Look at you he said
Exactly the earth
In the moment of tremors
Shaking and shivering
Lips fluttering
Like wings
Hands and legs trembling
I can see hot emotions
Flowing like lava
Through castles of glass
Breaking its way through
Blinking doors
What makes you shy of me
How do i come close to you
You make me feel afraid of me

Life Story

Every life tells a story
who writes the one?
Did I say I am a writer?
Do I write words, just Words?
I write on paper
Make o boat of write
the boat sets off in a pail
I smile at my life
And then
I laugh at me
Is that life?
What an absurd comparison of
A rope with a snake
Where is life?
Where is breath?
Where is movement?
Where is it
In a pail???
Or out in the ocean

Impressive doesn't impress
Keep it simple
My soul whispered
Touch the ground
Feel the dirt

As simple as that
Clap your hands
Slap your face
Hurt is the cost to wake
As simple as that
You can write big
Diamonds and pearls
For stones of words
I ask you my child
How genuine do you express
When you desire to impress
Write to express
Not just to impress
As simple as that

Shareef

Abdur

Rasheed

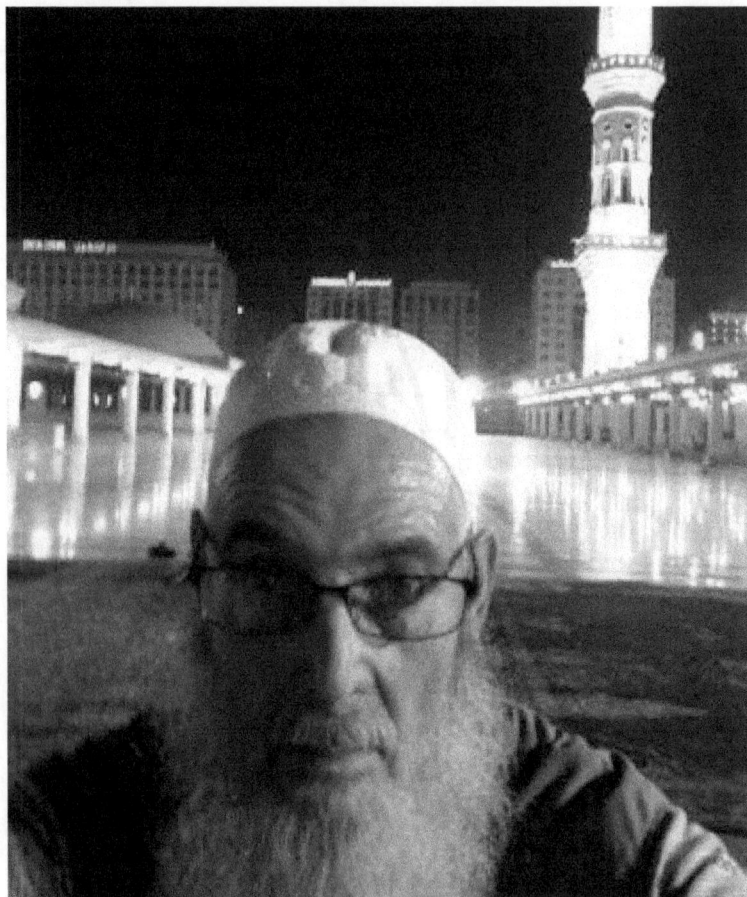

Shareef Abdur-Rasheed,AKA,Zakir Flo was born and raised in Brooklyn, New York. His education includes Brooklyn College, Suffolk County Community College and Makkah, Saudi Arabia. He is a Veteran of the Viet Nam era, where in 1969 he reverted to his now reverently embraced Islamic Faith. He is very active in the Islamic community and beyond with his teachings, activism and his humanity.

Shareef's spiritual expression comes through the persona of "Zakir Flo" . Zakir is Arabic for "To remind". Never silent, Shareef Abdur-Rasheed is always dropping science, love, consciousness and signs of the time in rhyme.

Shareef is the Patriarch of the Abdur-Rasheed Family with 9 Children (6 Sons and 3 Daughters) and 42 Grandchildren (24 Boys and 18 Girls).

For more information about Shareef,
contact or follow him at :

http://www.facebook.com/shareef.abdurrasheed1

http://zakirflo.wordpress.com/

http://www.innerchildpress.com/shareef-abdur-rasheed.php

https://www.facebook.com/pages/Muslim-Writers-Forum/370511683056503

orange..,

red, yellow, gold mellow
glow
radiant signs of glory
designed, created, painted
by the one and one (1)
only
he who has no needs
like getting lonely!
certainly neither sleep
nor slumber
is the architect of sweet
radiant summer
with its light lit life
and oh how the heat even
lingers into the night
something bout summer
days 'n' nights
something bout that feeling
zest for life!
want to feel rest of life
but even summer brings
test to life
with it's violence cutting deep
like butter with a ~~Hot~~ knife
hot days, hot nights..,

have elements that can and does
put and end to life
oooh how quick life can flip the
script
on any given day or night
having fun in the summer can
come with a steep price
when folk ultimately pay with
their life!
other then that fact, be carefull,
safe!
may your summer, day 'n' nights
find you 'n' yours in a peacefull,
protected, blessed state!.....,

Aameen!

food 4 thought!

Summer..,

comes on a slow burn
easin up on ya
feel the warmth of sun
feel the want for fun
brightness invigorates
zest for life vibrates
feelings swell to celebrate
mingling with people
awoken from slumber
exhibiting hunger for
summer
sunrays bring renewed
energy
come play in the sand with
me
hold my hand and walk with
me
let's relax 'n' talk about the
`~birds 'n' bees~`
sit with me under the star lit
tree
look deep in eyes
make love to me
soo great to be alive next to

you by my side
sharing love and the vibe
in the summertime!
so grand to soak in the sea
'n' sand
feeling the warmth of you next
to me
humans seeking feelings of
ecstasy
while sunrays and warm water
wash over me
wishing summer could always be
more then a memory of you
surreal!
memories of your hot body
next to mine in the summer,
summer, summertime!

food 4 thought!

Radiant..,

sun cuts through
slowly burns off
morning dew
source of warmth
for me and you
to lend a hand
agent to help nourish
replenish the land,
heal wounds,inspire
poems
wonders sometime
wander away from our
minds
as we look beyond or
back behind
trying to search for peace
of mind!
overlooking whats been right
there all the time
like good 'ol' simple sunshine!
never have to search far for
light when there's a time for
day, one for night!
so be patient soon the sun will
rise and bless you with light
take the darkness out your life!
see the "nur" in nourish?
that's light!
like life, to be relished!

food 4 thought!

Kimberly Burnham

An Integrative Medicine practitioner, Kimberly Burnham uses poetry, words, coaching and hands-on therapies to help you heal. A published poet in several Inner Child Press anthologies, including Healing Through Words and I Want My Poetry To, Kimberly is winner of SageUSA's story contest with a poem about her 2013 Hazon CrossUSA bicycle ride. She is writing The Journey Home about that 3000 mile expedition.

Now, you get to be her muse with a list of seven experiences you yearn for. She writes a poem as if already, you are feeling the exhilaration of living your dreams.

You can find Kimberly ...

http://www.KimberlyBurnhamPhD.com
http://www.linkedin.com/in/KimberlyBurnham
http://www.amazon.com/Kimberly-Burnham/e/B0054RZ4A0

Wildly Cultivated Boundaries

Nine weeks
from the seat of a bicycle
edges touching one
self ending who
before I was
crossing the land

Beginning
who am I
to be after
bumping up against
the duality
self and not self
recognition dawning
wheels turning
whirling
spinning the light

Consciousness
encompassing
challenging edges
where I meets you
apart of the whole
like sand and water
an imaginary line between
us

The field's border
wild culture joins in
diverse layers thriving
bathed in waves of possibility
creating one multitude
particles of experience

Reflections

Light reflecting off the river
blackberry flowers
on the imitating water
echoing images
of the Hazon cyclists
ahead

A mirror at a treacherous turn
on the path
a big silvery globe
above traffic extending sight
around the corner
catching the light
bouncing it to me

Clouds and shades of messy green
on the glassy pond
a glistening watering hole
brown cows oblivious
to what we are
reflecting into the world
on which we reflect

How does the light
bouncing off me
shimmering look
on the first
of many cross USA days

Vacillating

Between the satisfaction
joy in beautiful
sunny 90 mile rides
moose sightings,
beavers, cranes, trains
tiny yellow headed birds

There creeps in
despair on a hard day
wondering am I
insane to be
voluntarily bicycling
across
this country

Capturing me
with a magician's sleight of hand
beauty in the silver lined clouds
hanging like smoke
on the mountain tops
closing the distant Montana sky
warmth in the lushness
created by the rain
and prism angles
from the crown of the world

Noticing what you notice
as you slow down
on a journey
expectations shifting

like sand in water
with options inside moments
of confusion on the path

And optimistic again
watching the sunlight
leap off the river
a delicate gymnast
delighting in the huge raven
sighted, seen
observing a glimpse

Speeding up
information's intake
as you coast
downhill or
sense a tail wind's support
that day
life is good again
you think
knowing
life is always good
and there is beauty
to be captured everywhere

William

S.

Peters, Sr.

Bill's writing career spans a period quickly approaching 50 years. Being first Published in 1972, Bill has since went on to Author 28 additional Volumes of Poetry, Short Stories, etc., expressing his thoughts on matters of the Heart, Spirit, Consciousness and Humanity. His primary focus is that of Love, Peace and Understanding!

Bill is the Founding Director of Inner Child Enterprises as well as the Past Director of Publicity for Society Hill Music.

Bill says . . .

I have always likened Life to that of a Garden. So, for me, Life is simply about the Seeds we Sow and Nourish. All things we "Think and Do", will "Be" Cause and eventually manifest itself to being an "Effect" within our own personal "Existences" and "Experiences" . . . whether it be Fruit, Flowers, Weeds or Barren Landscapes! Bill highly regards the Fruits of his Labor and wishes that everyone would thus go on to plant "Lovely" Seeds on "Good Ground" in their own Gardens of Life!

to connect with Bill, he is all things Inner Child :
www.iaminnerchild.com

Personal Web Site
www.iamjustbill.com

the Spirit of Joy

the Spirit of Joy came to visit
her sister in my heart named Love
with dance and song and butterflies
the fruit from the heavens above

where all the children are singing
a ballad to each moment's bliss
embracing life's utter abundance
with a deep and soulful kiss

where days are never ending
and twinkling stars but yet no night
where all is seen as all is
for each heart bears it's own light

oh the gift imparted me
a remembrance of my way
that as a child of the "Magnificent One"
be bright and bonny and gay

and let the Spirit of Joy reside
and paint her rainbows in your heart
and love's promise will be fulfilled
and never let her part

. . . the Spirit of Joy . . .

Negril

on the north side of the island
walking towards West End
the Ocean's on my right side
there is nothing to defend

the waves languidly lapping
caressing my Here my Now
for Ego has surrendered
with reverence some way, some how

the Sun with love embraces
the divineness of all "BE"ing
the soft gentle breeze dusts off my lenses
and now my Soul is seeing

that all is One and One IS All
as my toes dig in the sand
i have escaped the confines of Self
and now i understand

if i but just let go and be
the limits do not exist
"i am" the genesis of what "i am"
be it anguish be it bliss

in . . . Negril . . .

so let the Sun Shine

the times i have fallen
i remember
but they are of no consequence
at this moment
for the joy of running
has overcome me

i give my self to the world of wonder
and i wonder as i wander
is this how
i used to feel
when i did not know
to give a damn ?

sitting here kicking it
in the sunshine of my life
i realize where the shade is
and when needed

i will take advantage
of this knowledge i thought needless,
but i accumulated it
in spite of my disdain
for class

and after the day is done
and bodies are weary
and with smiles of satisfaction
upon our faces,
me and the other Children of Creation
sleep peacefully
in expectation
for we know
That Joy Cometh In The Morning.

so let the Sun Shine

William S. Peters, Sr.

July

Features

~ * ~

Christena A. V. Williams

Dr. John R. Strum

Kolade Olanrewaju Freedom

Christena
A. V.
Williams

Christena A.V. Williams

Jamaican born Christena AV Williams is predicted to be a future revolutionist however she is a renowned poet and Author of Pearls among stones published by Canadian, Brian Wixon.

She dabbles in philosophy and history. Christena began writing at age ten, and ten years later published her first collection of poetry. This eventually earned her one of the most prestigious awards ever given to youths in Jamaica, The Prime Ministers National Youth Awards in excellence. Christena is a phenomenal gift and feels she is destined and determined to share her words with the hearts of humanity. She is committed to write for the hopeless and share wisdom from which God speaks through her while spilling ink on paper.

Christena hopes to inspire other individuals especially her generation to believe and achieve their dreams. She hopes one day to have her own publishing company. There is so much this young woman hopes to achieve and share with others. One of her greatest visions is for Jamaica and Jamaicans to return to place of paradise. This poets greatest inspiration is her Mother. Her Father left her when she was one year old her Mother a strong black woman of whom she loves and emulates worked very hard that she may know the importance of perseverance, love, dedication, hard work and that dreams are not impossible however possible to attain.

Links

http://www.blurb.com/b/4148458-pearls-among-stones
http://jamaica-gleaner.com/gleaner/20140427/arts/arts2.html
http://jamaica-gleaner.com/gleaner/20140507/ent/ent1.html
http://www.amazon.com/The-dVerse-Anthology-Voices-Contemporary/dp/1939832012
https://www.facebook.com/worldclasspoet

Hope is a thing with wings

Hope is driven by fear and by defeat

It is a feeling of optimism Hope is a bird with bad wings

Giving it courage to fly and to soar to overcome what is

missing

Hope is a thing with wings.

Hope makes you dream of what seems unrealistic

It is a feeling of over zealousness

New ideas

A new day

It bubbles in you like burning volcanic eruptions

It is like a metaphorical poem

Hope is a thing with wings.

Each day I wake, I see the clouds

Beautiful

Birds fly limitlessly

The trees flow like Musical notes on a piano

From these creations, I know hope is a thing with wings.

Survival

I was born in a city

Where there is no love, no unity

I was born in a country

Where disease and hunger bites as if a mosquito was

sucking your

Blood

I was born in a world

Where my colour means segregation

I was born in a land

Where hardship lies

Where power means corruption

Where killing means surviving

I was born in a home

Where one bed means five people

Where one slice of bread means five bellies

I was born in a universe where surviving means giving up

your life

For the next generation to be free.

Quench my thirst

You whisper sweet words
I feel your lust driven by sexual thoughts
You pluck my chord
Play me like a violin
String by string,

Seductively driving me insane
Setting my whole body in motion
I long to be entangled in you like a web
Kissing your lips and turning you red
Take a trip in my land and pleasure me.

Take me to the heights of climax
These desires filling you
You need not to hide it like Victoria's secret
However, reveal for I wish for you to massage
Relieve, touching every pressure point.

I Drank poetry

Bartender
Pour me some more
Let me stumble through the back door
Let the police
Smell the poignant aroma of rhythm and blues
Collide with my Genius creative expression
Handcuff me for resisting being silent
Check my breath for the bubbles of a drunken poet
Spitting up words and rhymes
Expressively with profanity of poetry
Charge me with intoxication
Verbal sensation
Before the judge
I plead guilty
Poetic confinement recommended
On the walls, I write art
Painting out the graffiti of the prisoner's thoughts
And colouring with poetic expressions

Bartender
Pour me some more
Until my cup overflows
I just cannot get enough
Let this liquor become embedded in my arteries and lungs
Let it be in my very DNA
Let it flow through my blood and veins
Through my heart and mind
Let it be hypnosis for my dreams
I drank poetry and it tastes delicious.

Revolutionary minds

I want you to think positive today
Speak up when you have something to say
Stand up and let your voice be heard
Whenever injustice knocks at your door
Do not be afraid to cry out for mercy
Do not be afraid to cry so the world may be at your knees.

Do not be afraid to be vocal
Whether foreign or local
Do not be afraid to challenge the stagnant system
Whether by voice or by the written work
Let our hearts beat as one with the Congo rhythm
Sing out The great reggae legend philosophy
Bob Marley
One Love, One hearts lets get together and feel all right
I and I is a woman of righteousness
Everywhere me step Jah bless.

Me radical
Every vagabond has to scatter as the power under which is
dwell is internalized
Out of me the almighty specialized and their wicked cult
cannot suffice
So open up your eyes
Please do realize
Take away the cobwebs and remove the mask of disguise
See I prophecy
Paint away the graffiti of one's mind
Remove the zinc fences and cardboard boxes
That tries to manipulate

See God
See the devil when he masquerades
Realize his plan
His advocates and be aware.

It is a physical
A spiritual warfare
Soldiers
Put on your armour
Prepare for war
Keep your mind open
Keep it secure
The gateways to your soul
Protect it with spiritual intervention
If you don't
Illusion
Delusion
Difficult situation
Under the system's manipulation
Hold an herbal, spiritual meditation
And revolutionized
Modernized this ya mind.

Christena A.V. Williams

Dr. John
R.
Strum
(Bob)

Dr. John R. Strum

Dr. John R. Strum aka Bob is an Passionate and Avid Writer / Poet with a professional background in Psychiatry.

Bob employs all aspects of his experiences and his formal education in the examination of many subjects. Within the weaving of his lines and verse there is sometime some very subtle yet profound insights he lends to the reader which set them on a path of their own discovery of self as they contemplate and reflect on Bob's subject matter and unique perspectives.

All of Bob's work may appear to be borne of his own journey, however the astute reader will see pieces of themselves dancing in the merrily in the metaphors and adjectives. Have fun . . . may your journey be a richly rewarding as the wonderful poetry of Dr. John R. Strum.

Reminiscing

As we're walking down Lake Charles Listening to
The Louisiana Jazz greats Trombone Shorty,
Louis Satchmo Armstrong and the legends...
Your scent is like , walking into a fresh summers
Bath in the back woods of the Louisiana Bayou...

The sweet smell of gumbo prepared in cousin
Josephine's kitchen where customers would come
To get a free samples of it, teasingly passes, by
My direction as we're holding hands... I smile
Reminiscing of you~lifting me off my feet up

Into your masculine muscular arms ...I gazed
At the sexiest way the white of your teeth
Brings the pride and joy of your smile
Can make a crowd at the Saints game thinking
They've won before the game ever began~

You're such a rare gentleman and a fine piece of art
Look at you~with your seersucker powder blue shirt
Open for the cool summers breeze off the Bayou's
And Lakes...sleeves and khaki's rolled up your arms
And Legs just enough to walk through the scenic
Prairie byways~

The look on your face you give me can melt my heart
Which renders my surrendering every moment of
Me to you, as we kiss...you held my chin as delicately
And tenderly leaving me with a sweet erotic heart
Pounding daydreaming of a moment to be imaged for

Our next sentimental journey...you open up the door
For me from your beautiful 1941 Studebaker Lark
Convertible...that automobile still speaks
Long time memories of us...You walk around the back
flirtatiously touching the curves of the vehicle never

Taking your big dreamy bedroom eyes off me
As I open the driver side door, your eyes fall down
Upon my bosom, from leaning too far over releasing
The door handle...I smile... as you drive away
You take my left hand, ever so gently caressing it

Glancing at the 5 carat diamond ring given by you
From your Mother for your future bride to be
You pull me close to you while we ride with
Anticipation of Love pondering inside my heart
Of our trip to the next destination...(to be con't.)

Dr. John R. Strum

Loving You In The Fall

I love when the Fall leaves
Free fall flows from the trees
Twirls down on our heads, face
And sweaters
It brings out the warm Happiness
Inside our Joyful Hearts of Love
we run in the bustling piles of
Fallen leaves Vibrant bursting
Colors of "Mother Earth's" canvas
painting our picture in Awesome
Technicolor of what love like ours
Has to show
the Spiritual light Of the universe
Is a guiding light to the Greatness
In our lives that we have to give
Not only for Us, but for All
You lift me so high above the
Clouds is where I lay
I love your Big Bear Hugs
When You run up behind me
So safe and cozy
Wrapped inside your arms
Don't let me go, let's hold on
To this moment and close our eyes
Smell the fall aroma of Cantaloupes
Pumpkins, and Cranberries
As I face you and look into your
Face, I know, this is the place
I want to live throughout the rest
Of my Wonderfully Blessed Days
With ...."YOU"~

I Wrote "Nice" Today

I wrote Beautiful today ~I wrote about the sunrise
and made the moon hide, filled the air with butterflies
and Honeysuckle, while birds chirped and sang as they
flew away into the fresh smell of evergreen

I wrote Happy today, watching the neighbors get out for
church and the football teams were huddled up
ice cream trucks ringing their bells for children with tiny
giggles, snotty noses and bouncy pigtails

I wrote Romantic today, a cute young couple sitting on
the edge of a fountain of cupids with arrows firing water
while they make future plans of marriage ahead
and elderly guys making check mate on one another
for the second week straight

I wrote Passionate today, I painted a picture of a nude
couple
that had no curtains or blinds to hide from, he was giving
her
a Mandarin Coconut Massage, touching every smooth, soft,
curved mound, fingers and toes...were all tasty and liked
by him...hmmm, he makes me want some of his Mandarin
Coconut Massage Oils...
Yes, I painted him Passionately beautiful
today and loved every touch of It ~

Dr. John R. Strum

You made me Love You

I admired everything about him
his charm was so much to adore.
He enlightened my heart
as if a halo of warm light traced my silhouette
He made a smile appear upon my face
that I'd never seen since two years back
He told me things that no one else would know
about him at that time
I fell head over heels
of the plans we made for the future
I heard of all his dreams
I melted into his life with our hands held close
He took care of my emotions
because he said to trust him
He caressed my ego
my heart no longer ached from the pain in my life
that i suffered from my past , because at last
our love was one
he held me so dear to his heart from a thousand
miles away ...

Addicted To You

I wake up this morning
Your eyes penetrating mine
I kiss your lips, embracing me
Is all the wanting of you I crave
Everyday with you is absolute
Ecstasy
I want you more today then
Yesterday, and twice as much
Hungering for you tomorrow
You open my world by twirling
My pearl of satisfying sensual
Touches of pulsating vibrations
You tantalize my senses
You devour every moment of my
Thoughts when I think of you
I can't, Turn away I'm addicted
To you, you keep the fire burning
Through me feeling me up
with Passion in my soul
Your caresses like no other
you love me wrapped around
Your every daydream
Of you making love to me with
those pillow soft screams
Satisfying you, is my life
With you never to have you
yearning because you whispered
Bella' you're my Eternity
So I'll continue to take you
Through phases of seductions
While you embrace me saying,
"I'm Addicted to You"

Dr. John R. Strum

Kolade
Olanrewaju
Freedom

Kolade O. Freedom

Kolade Olanrewaju (Freedom) was born in the early 90s in Osogbo, the capital of Osun State, Nigeria. He began writing creatively as a child who fell in love with the African literature. His literary works have appeared in diverse global charity anthologies, magazines, websites and blogs. He was named a Pentasi B. Inspirational Poet in Philippines for the year 2013 as well as the winner of the first edition of UK's Write Share Be Read Poetry Competition-Category A. He is also an Awardee of Janet P. Caldwell's Essay Contest underwritten by Inner Child Press (USA).

He has authored two poetry collections titled 'My First Poetry Book' and 'The Light Bearer'. He currently resides in Lagos where he weaves words to educate and entertain his readers.

Kolade O. Freedom

I Won Myself

Dust kissed the sole of my feet
As I trod upon the ground valiantly
A gargantuan task was set before me
I peered into my heart
And courage was visible
I peeked at a mirror
And I saw a fidgeting image
Whose image was it?

I battled in a bottle
Filled with mixture of fear and courage
I had to sieve
Or subdue one for the other
But every attempt to implement
The element of decisiveness
Left me sitting on a fence.

The battle called unto me
When I refused to confront
It drew nigh
Barking like a dog
Afflicted with insanity
I was humming
Yes, I was
Tension at attention
But fear was thrown in detention.

Courage assaulted fear within me
I pulled away from despair
I repaired the damaged faith
By damaging self-pity.

Joy was ignited
When worries were switched off
My soul freed
My body freed
I had won the greatest battle
I won myself to be myself.

It Is Not Over

Toiling all night long

Without a joyous song

To delete the gloominess

That has engulfed my soul.

Flapping my wings incessantly

Without flying off the spot

That cages me like a bird.

Weeping at the tomb of fate

Without a tear dropping off

The cloudy eyes of faith.

Through Poetry

Through poetry;

The pains will be chased away

Sad memories will be laid to rest

Comfort will be dispensed

As air for all to inhale.

Through poetry;

The mountains shall crumble

The lousy storm will be silenced

Cries parading on faces will be dried

Hearts that bleed will clot.

Kolade O. Freedom

Pity Us In Our Pit

We wail as we sail in this ship
Captained by melancholy
Earnestly pleading to be bailed
While we cuff our hands
But tear our mouth
To voice our grief.

Saddening!
The clueless present squeaks
As the thorny past chokes our future
Ironically, we are the diggers of our own doom,
The inventors of evil that booms.

Ah, Injustice builds a skyscraper
On a land treacherously sold
By the Jewish Judas in us
We scream- bring back our girls
While we stink of hypocrisy.

As hens besieged by hawks,
We flap our wings
When they ought to serve
As cloaks for our chicks.

The world will hear us not
But the muffled cries
Of our distressed girls.

Help can be sporadically
Shot at us like bullets
As long as the future
Is preserved as a seed
To blossom at the bosom
Of a seaside Palm tree.

#BringBackOurGirls

Kolade O. Freedom

I Once Snubbed The Pen

Not once have I seen an ocean
Mourning the loss of its body
Nor a star appealing to the sky
To have a lamp to shine.

Not once have I begged
To wield the pen to pen;
Blame me not for being haughty
The engines fascinated me more.

Not once have I prevailed
Over dictatorial destiny;
I chose to snub the pen
But ended up being a poet.

Other

Anthological

works by

Inner Child Press, ltd.

www.innerchildpress.com

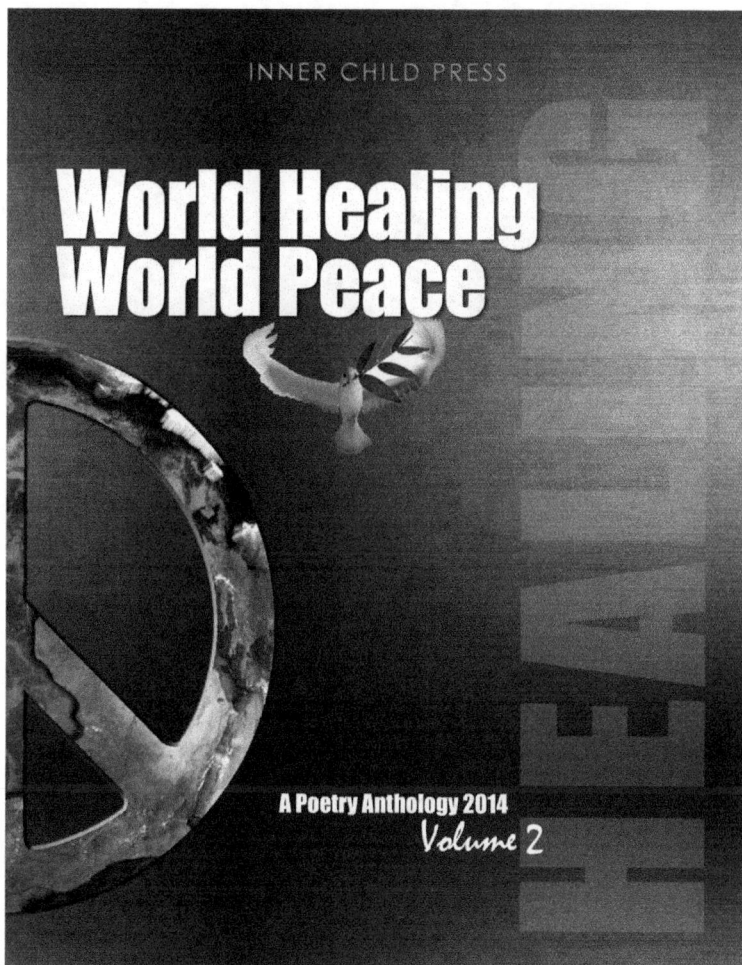

INNER CHILD PRESS

World Healing
World Peace

A Poetry Anthology 2014
Volume 2

HEALING

the year of the poet

May 2014

May's Featured Poets

ReeCee
Joski the Poet
Shannon Stanton

Dedicated To our Children

The Poetry Posse

Jamie Bond
Gail Weston Shazor
Albert 'Infinite' Carrasco
Siddartha Beth Pierce
Janet P. Caldwell
June 'Bugg' Barefield
Debbie M. Allen
Tony Henninger
Joe DeVerbal Minddancer
Robert Gibbons
Neetu Wali
Shareef Abdur-Rasheed
Kimberly Burnham
William S. Peters, Sr.

Lily of the Valley

Inner Child Press
Anthologies

the Year of the Poet

April 2014

The Poetry Posse

Jamie Bond
Gail Weston Shazor
Albert 'Infinite' Carrasco
Siddartha Beth Pierce
Janet P. Caldwell
June 'Bugg' Barefield
Debbie M. Allen
Tony Henninger
Joe DaVerbal Minddancer
Robert Gibbons
Neetu Wali
Shareef Abdur-Rasheed
Kimberly Burnham
William S. Peters, Sr.

Our April Featured Poets
Fahredin Shehu
Martina Reisz Newberry
Justin Blackburn
Monte Smith

Sweet Pea

celebrating international poetry month

the Year of the Poet

The Poetry Posse   March 2014

Jamie Boud
Gail Weston Shazor
Albert 'Infinite' Carrasco
Siddartha Beth Pierce
Janet P. Caldwell
June 'Bugg' Barefield
Debbie M. Allen
Tony Henninger
Joe DaVerbal Minddancer
Robert Gibbons
Neetu Wali
Shareef Abdur-Rasheed
Kimberly Burnham
William S. Peters, Sr.

daffodil

Our March Featured Poets

Alicia C. Cooper & hülya yılmaz

Inner Child Press
Anthologies

the Year of the Poet

February 2014

violets

The Poetry Posse

Jamie Bond
Gail Weston Shazor
Albert 'Infinite' Carrasco
Siddartha Beth Pierce
Janet P. Caldwell
June 'Bugg' Barefield
Debbie M. Allen
Tony Henninger
Joe DaVerbal Minddancer
Robert Gibbons
Neetu Wali
Shareef Abdur-Rasheed
William S. Peters, Sr.

Our February Features

Teresa E. Gallion & Robert Gibson

The Year of the Poet
January 2014

The Poetry Posse

Jamie Bond
Gail Weston Shazor
Albert 'Infinite' Carrasco
Siddartha Beth Pierce
Janet P. Caldwell
June 'Bugg' Barefield
Debbie M. Allen
Tony Henninger
Joe DaVerbal Minddancer
Robert Gibbons
Neetu Wali
Shareef Abdur-Rasheed
William S. Peters, Sr.

Carnation

Our January Feature
Terri L. Johnson

Mandela

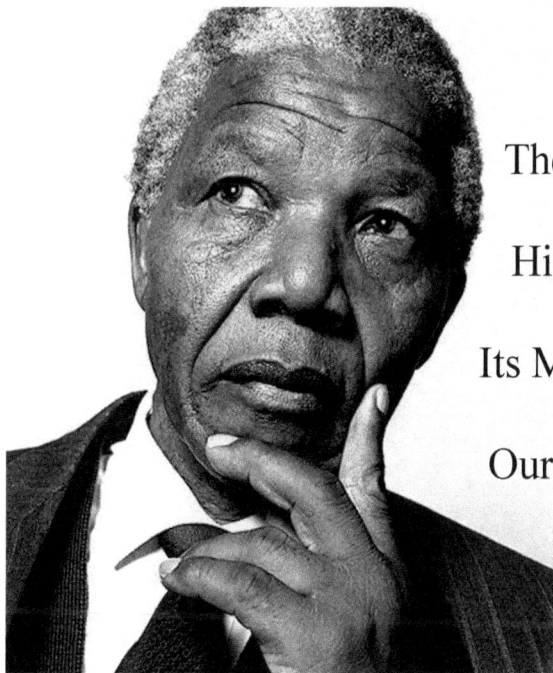

The Man

His Life

Its Meaning

Our Words

Poetry . . . Commentary & Stories
The Anthological Writers

Inner Child Press
Anthologies

A GATHERING OF WORDS

POETRY & COMMENTARY
FOR
TRAYVON MARTIN

Inner Child Press
Anthologies

World Healing
World Peace

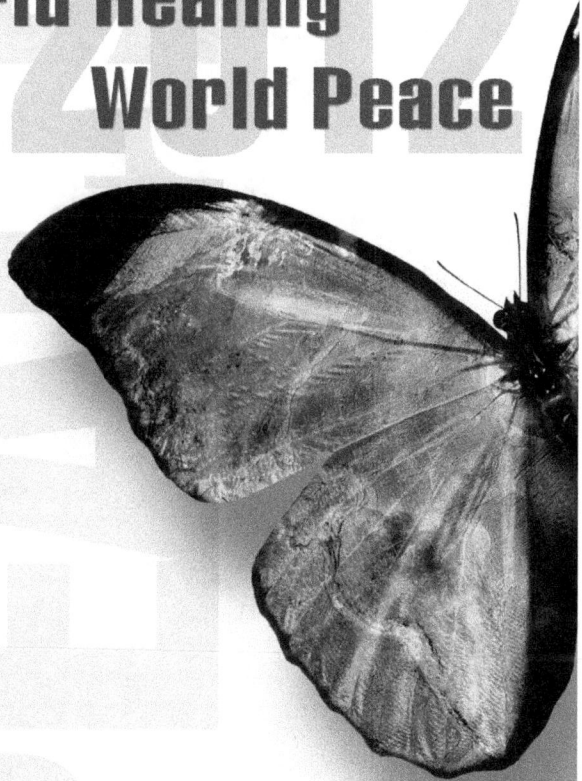

A POETRY ANTHOLOGY
Volume 1

Inner Child Press
Anthologies

2012

World Healing
World Peace

HEALING

A POETRY ANTHOLOGY
Volume 2

healing through words

Poetry ... Prose ... Prayer ... Stories

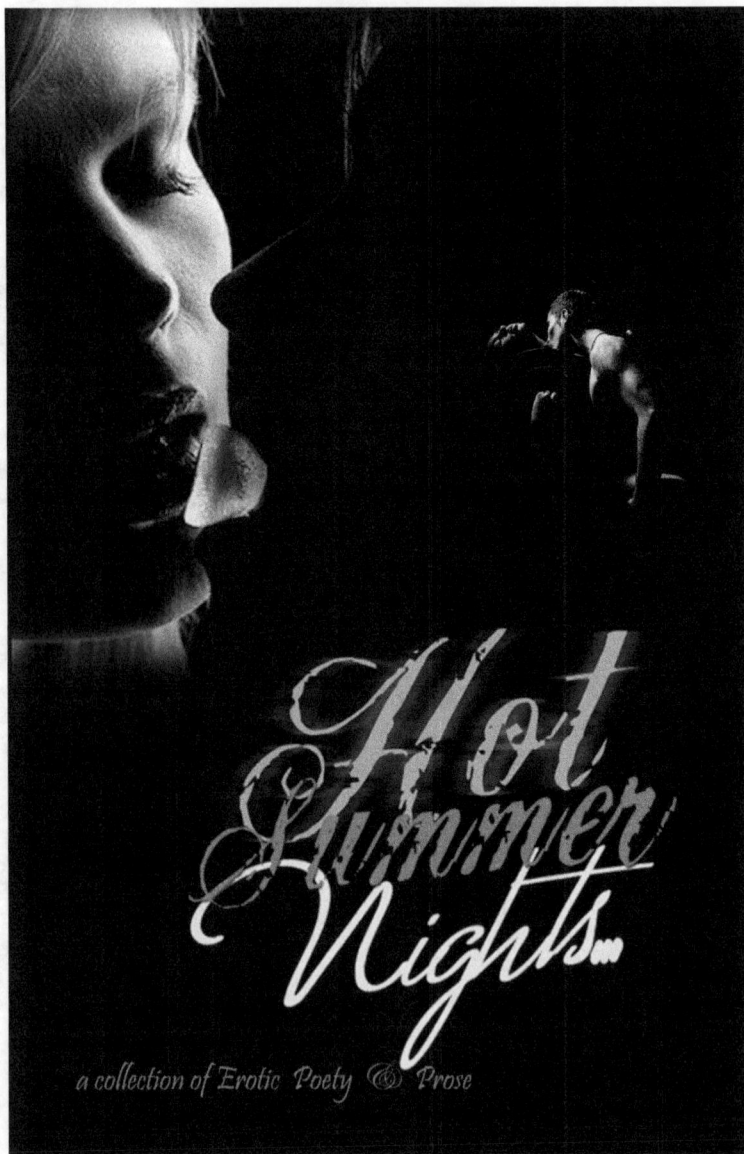

Hot Summer Nights...

a collection of Erotic Poetry & Prose

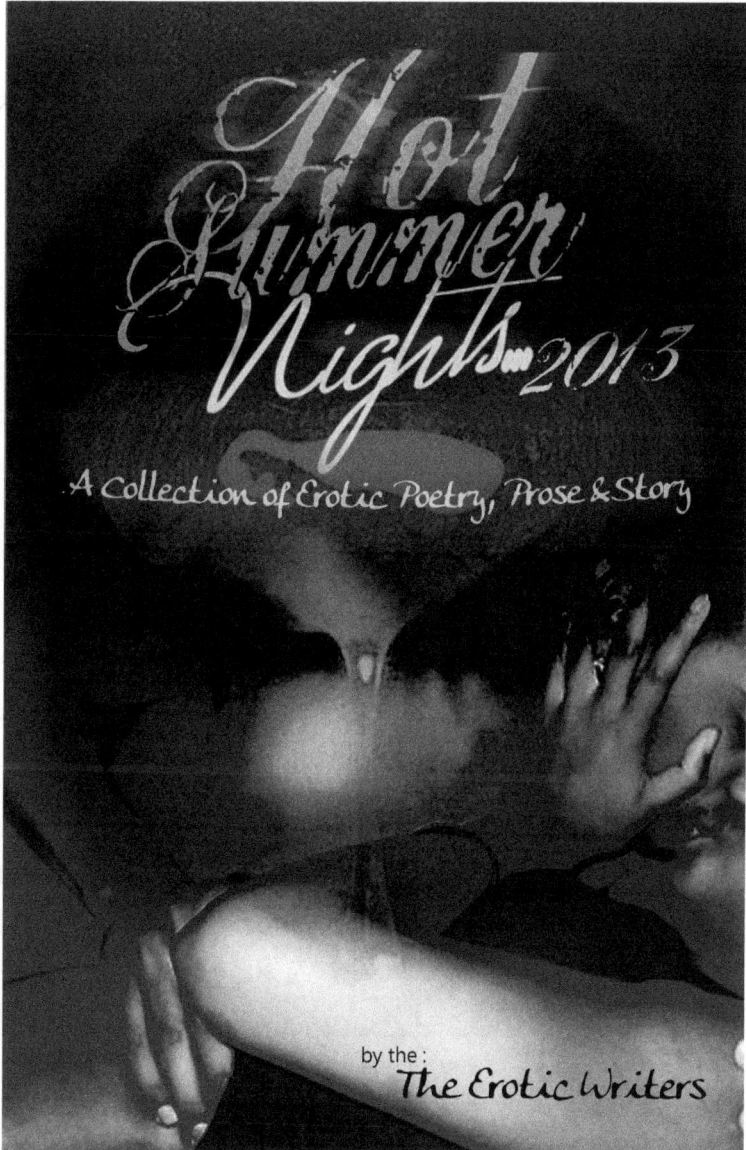

Hot Summer Nights... 2013

A Collection of Erotic Poetry, Prose & Story

by the :
The Erotic Writers

the

Valentine's Day

Anthology

poetry . . . prose & stories of love

The Love Writers

Inner Child Press
Anthologies

i

want my

PoEtRy

to . . .

a collection of the Voices of Many inspired by . . .

Monte Smith

Inner Child Press Anthologies

a collection of the Voices of Many inspired by ...

Monte Smith

 i

want my

PoEtRy

to . . .

volume II

11 Words

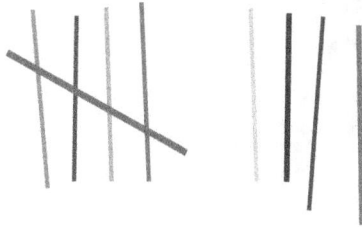

(9 lines . . .)

for those who are challenged

an anthology of Poetry inspired by . . .

Poetry Dancer

Inner Child Press
Anthologies

a
Poetically
Spoken
Anthology
volume I
Collector's Edition

Inner Child Press
Anthologies

and there is much, much more !

visit . . .

http://www.innerchildpress.com
/anthologies-sales-special.php

Also check out our Authors and
all the wonderful Books
Available at :

http://www.innerchildpress.com
/the-book-store.php

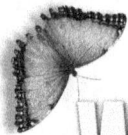

www.worldhealingworldpeacepoetry.com

Inner Child Press
Anthologies

Tee Shirts & Hats

4

Sale

Anthologies for Sale

WORLD HEALING ~ WORLD PEACE

$ 20.00

SMALL * MED. * LARGE * XL * XXL

www.worldhealingworldpeacepoetry.com

Tee Shirts for Sale

$ 22.00

http://www.innerchildpress.com/the-year-of-the-poet.php

COMBOS

$ 25.00

SMALL * MED. * LARGE * XL * XXL

FOR INTERNATIONAL POETRY MONTH ONLY

www.worldhealingworldpeacepoetry.com

Tee Shirts for Sale

COMBOS

$ 40.00

SMALL * MED. * LARGE * XL * XXL

http://www.innerchildpress.com/the-year-of-the-poet.php

Anthologies for Sale

COMBOS

$ 50.00

SMALL * MED. * LARGE * XL * XXL

http://www.innerchildpress.com/the-year-of-the-poet.php

180

This Anthological Publication
is underwritten solely by

Inner Child Press

Inner Child Press is a Publishing Company
Founded and Operated by Writers. Our personal
publishing experiences provides us an intimate
understanding of the sometimes daunting
challenges Writers, New and Seasoned may face in
the Business of Publishing and Marketing their
Creative "Written Work".

For more Information

Inner Child Press

www.innerchildpress.com

FINI